My Odyssey

My Odyssey

Stories, Poems, and Verse

Joseph Kennedy

iUniverse, Inc.
Bloomington

My Odyssey
Stories, Poems, and Verse

iUniverse books may be ordered through booksellers or by contacting:

iUniverse
1663 Liberty Drive
Bloomington, IN 47403
www.iuniverse.com
1-800-Authors (1-800-288-4677)

ISBN: 978-1-4620-3662-2 (sc)
ISBN: 978-1-4620-3663-9 (hc)
ISBN: 978-1-4620-3664-6 (ebk)

Library of Congress Control Number: 2011912103

Printed in the United States of America

iUniverse rev. date:11/11/2011

Acknowledgments go to my family, friends, and teachers. That includes those teachers in and outside of the classroom, as well as my students. I would like to thank the people at iUniverse for their time and patience. Without their help, this effort could neither have begun nor concluded.

CONTENTS

Introduction

This collection is organized chronologically. In arranging the works this way, I'm inviting you to watch as my creative voice develops through my odyssey. I'm attempting to show growth, change, and adaptation, both obvious and subtle. What I found striking about preparing this book is that it reacquainted me with who I am. I can remember all the works despite the passage of time. Peruse at your leisure. I'm fortunate to have been able to write, and I hope that you also travel well in your odyssey.

1960S

The Mistake

(short story assignment from high school)

Kevin Kennedy, a spry young lad of nine, readied himself to depart for Glennville. *It's gonna be swell to get away from Bakersfield for awhile*, thought Kevin as he finished putting his last pair of socks in his duffle bag. Beat-up and battered as the duffle was, it still held food, matches, and other essentials superbly. *Good day*, he thought, and it was. Cloudless, cool, and with a little breeze set off this beautiful Friday in June. He walked over to his bed and stretched out full length on it.

He lay on his bed and pondered over what had happened the previous evening. He had come in late for dinner last night. This happened more than once; but when he gave his reason, that was the straw that had broken the camel's back.

"Hi, Mom. Hi, Dad," he called out.

"Why are ya late, son?" asked his dad with some concern in his voice.

"Over at Jamie's," stated Kevin shortly.

"What were you doing that was so important that it couldn't wait until tomorrow?"

"Playin' in his tree house."

"Son, I've told you before to be home in time for dinner. I guess tellin' won't do it, so you'll go to bed without any dinner tonight," stated his father gently but firmly.

After Kevin had gone to bed, Jo Kennedy said her first words of the evening. "Did you have to be so rough on him, Jim?"

"Jo, if it had been the first time, I'd have let it go. But this is about the fifth time it's happened." Jo left the matter at that.

Meanwhile, upstairs, Kevin was thinking up a way to get around this event. *I'll run away,* he concluded exuberantly.

So, here he was, in a high-spirited mood, ready to tackle anything that life presented to him. He got up from his reclining position and gazed into the full-length mirror neatly screwed into the closet door. The picture was that of a boy about 4'4", blue eyes, and strawberry blond hair. He was frail, weighing only seventy-seven pounds.

Suddenly, he remembered that Jamie, Dave, and Steve were waiting for him to get them. He rushed over to Steve's house, three houses from his. The lot looked deserted, but he knocked anyway. A Negro woman, the size of one of the football players he had seen on television, answered the door.

"Is Steve Burns there?" he inquired, trembling.

"Naw, son, they left fo' Los Angeles this morning."

"Oh, thanks."

As Kevin turned on his way to Dave Goni's house, he wondered who or what a Los Angeles was and if it were poisonous. *No matter,* he thought. He dismissed the matter hurriedly as he approached the Goni residence. He rang the bell. The stillness that followed bothered him. Ringing three more times with no answer, he left downcast. *Jamie just has gotta be home,* he thought. But, as at the other two stops, Jamie had vacated the premises.

Dejectedly, Kevin turned on his way northward toward Glennville. Using the Glennville-Woody Road, the journey was still going to take forty miles. But he had forgotten his good old fishing pole. So carefully he entered the house, grabbed his fishing pole, and crept out again. At least he thought he was creeping out. Approximately four pairs of eyes peeped from corners all over the house. The eyes of Dave, Steve, and Jamie, all handsome characters of eight years apiece, peered from the corner of the dining room. The other set belonged to Mrs. Kennedy, who was gazing intently from the bedroom.

"Come back into the kitchen and finish your story over some cookies and milk," said Mrs. Kennedy excitedly.

Sitting down at the banquet-size table, Jamie retold their story.

"Kevin came over after school Thursday night and asked me if I wanted to run away, to which I said yes. Then I asked how long we'd be gone. He said he didn't know. After that, he told me to call Steve and Dave and ask them if they wanted to, too."

"What kept you from going?" inquired Mrs. Kennedy.

"I didn't want to go," said Jamie, a fair-skinned boy.

"Why didn't you go?" asked Mrs. Kennedy, directing her line of questioning to Steve.

"Well, Mrs. K., Mom and Dad said no, and I really didn't want—"

"Where were you when he went after you to—" she interrupted.

"Huh?" Steve interrupted in return.

"You said Dolly, the maid, told you a boy came for you around 9:00 a.m. I hope the boy was Kevin," she said nervously.

"Oh, yeah. I told Dolly to say we'd went to Los Angeles," said Steve, grinning in a manner that showed the blank spaces where two front teeth were supposed to be.

"And you, Dave?" she queried.

"I just left the house and since Mom and Dad were working, nobody would've answered," the dark-skinned boy replied.

"Excellent," commended Jo.

After the three boys had gone home, Jo Kennedy gave out with a little chuckle. "I'll bet the first place he went was Glennville," she said aloud. Then, bursting into laughter, she blurted, "I've gotta tell Jim." Coming into seriousness for a moment, she figured that it would be wise to call Mrs. Kennedy (Jim's mother) just in case Kevin made it. After calling her, Jo decided to call Jane Burns to see if she and Steve wanted to take a ride to see where Kevin was.

"Hello, Jane? Would you check on Kevin?"

"Sure, Jo, when?"

"No big hurry, but how about within the next two hours?"

"Fine with me," replied Jane.

"Thanks," said Mrs. Kennedy ending the conversation.

Ten miles north, Kevin was sitting down to a hastily prepared lunch of beans and bread. He hadn't had much time to pack a lot of food, since his mom had come down the stairs and he had had to make a quick retreat out the back door. He thought surely his mom had seen him, but she never came back up to his bedroom that morning to ask him why he was down there, so she must have been looking the other way. At least that was what he thought. As he pulled his canteen from his duffle bag, he wondered if they were missing him. "They should be, 'cause I'm missing them," he sobbed. "Oh, I can make it without 'em," he said, talking to no one in particular. Picking up his things and continuing for about a mile, he searched for a shaded area in which he could lie down. He found a clear, grassy hill. It looked so inviting that he overlooked the fact that there was no tree. He ascended the hill, just off the road, shed all baggage, and went to sleep.

Ten minutes later, Jane and Steve Burns passed the exact spot where Kevin lay.

"That's Kev," shouted Steve.

"Ssh!" reprimanded Mrs. Burns.

Making a U-turn further up the road, the Burns' car headed for Bakersfield.

Arriving home, Mrs. Burns immediately called the Kennedy residence. "Safe and sound," boomed Mrs. Burns.

"Where?" Jo queried.

"About five or six miles north," Mrs. Burns replied.

"Good. Thanks for going up there, Jane," Jo said graciously.

"That's alright, Jo. Do you want me to take a look tomorrow?" she asked politely.

"No, Jane, I think I'll ask Joy Schauss (Jamie's mom) if she'll go. Thanks for all you've done."

"You're welcome—see you later." With that, Jane hung up. Then Jo dialed the Schauss home.

"Joy, could you stop by my house tomorrow? I have something to ask you," began Jo.

"Who is this and why can't you tell me now?" Joy asked almost simultaneously.

"One at a time. First, this is Jo Kennedy—second, I'd rather tell you in person."

"How are you, Jo? You're not exactly talking to my spirit, ya know," she joked.

"Okay, I'll ask you now, then. Would you mind taking a trip to see where Kevin is tomorrow?"

"No, I wouldn't mind—where do I have to go?" Joy asked suspiciously.

"Glennville," Jo said quickly.

"Glennville?! I'm sure glad you're a friend, Jo," she said exhaustedly. "How'd he get up there?" she asked.

"I'll tell you tomorrow," she answered, taking for granted that Joy was coming over the next day.

"Fair enough," Joy answered. "I'll be over about noon tomorrow. See you then." Joy's line clicked.

The next day, Saturday, June 13, Joy was true to her word. Arriving at exactly noon, she heard the story that Jamie had failed to tell her. On hearing the exchange of conversation between his wife and Joy, Jim Kennedy asked, "Have I missed out on something?"

At seeing the innocent expression on her husband's face, Jo burst into laughter. After recovering her composure, she replied, "Honey, you sure have. I'll tell you later."

After fixing the date to pick Kevin up as Sunday, June 14, Joy left to check on him.

As Jo explained the story to her husband, he thought of the incident that had occasioned the trip. He had it coming to him, Jim concluded. When Jo finished, he said, "I'll pick him up tomorrow evening."

Joy reported that evening that Kevin had traveled about five or six more miles than Friday. "He's finished about a quarter of his journey," Joy said authoritatively.

By now, Kevin was missing his parents wholeheartedly. But something inside of him told him not to cry. The pride with which he had started out was about half gone, but the remaining half was enough to tell him not to go home.

Sunday evening was a normal one for the Kennedys. It included the big Sunday meal, recreation, and television until about eight o'clock. Over a piece of apple pie and some coffee, Jo said suddenly, "Don't forget Kevin, dear."

"I've gotta work tomorrow, hon," replied Jim helplessly.

"But you said you'd get him tonight," Jo stated, for the first time with a note of concern in her voice.

"He'll have to wait until tomorrow," Jim answered decisively.

Jo looked down dejectedly at the floor, as if she could find some sympathy hidden in the waxed linoleum. Jim finished his pie, walked over to her, and lifted her chin so that their eyes met. "Honey, I'll get him tomorrow," he said gently.

"Promise?" Jo asked with a smile.

"Promise," Jim replied sincerely.

They sealed their promise with a kiss.

By Sunday, Kevin had gone as far as Poso Creek and was preparing his pole to do some fishing. He had just eaten lunch, but was already thinking of dinner. Slipping his line into the water, Kevin's hopes for catching a fish or two were high. After about ten minutes in the water, the pole began to jiggle. Kevin tried to reel the catch in, but whatever was on the other end of the line was stronger. The hook snapped free of the line and the opponent on the other end swam away with it in his mouth. *Bet he was a big 'un*, thought Kevin excitedly. Attaching a new hook to the line, he tried again. This time, he reeled in a tidbit about 2 ½" in length. "You're too small," he whispered, looking the fish straight in the eye. Throwing the morsel back in the creek, he was determined to try once again. The fish that bit the line this time was no shrimp. Trying with all his might to reel it in, he had the fish less than two feet from him. Then the pole broke from the strain of the battle. Kevin tried diving in after it, but all he was able to get was a few scrapes and cuts since the creek was not deep enough to permit diving. He was, however, thoroughly soaked.

He walked back to dry land and gazed at his forlorn-looking fishing pole, not because it had cost fifteen dollars, but because it had been his only way of catching anything to eat. Now what was he going to do? "Ah!" he remembered. "I've got a two-day-old cheese sandwich somewhere in my duffle bag. Ech! Not very good but it's food," he decided. So about 7:00 p.m., he ate his mildewy but filling cheese sandwich.

Monday evening, the Kennedys ate dinner as soon as Jim came home from work. At 6:00 p.m. they left, taking the same road that their son had taken.

Kevin was checking his supplies and found out he had enough food and drink for about two more meals, if that many. He didn't want to go home, but if the chance presented itself, it wasn't likely to be ignored. With nothing else to do and some sleep to catch up on, Kevin sank into restful slumber.

Kevin had been asleep about fifteen minutes when a white Chevrolet station wagon arrived on the hill overlooking Poso Creek.

"There he is!" Jo exclaimed.

Jim's mind was temporarily a thousand miles away. He was looking at the magnificent sunset which, because of their locale and the change to Pacific Daylight Time, was lingering in the sky.

"Jim? Jim!" Mrs. Kennedy said curiously.

"Huh?" Jim replied absently.

"Honey, go down and get Kevin," she said anxiously.

"Okay."

Slowly, as if in a trance, Jim went to where he saw Kevin. "Ah, this brings back memories," Jim said to himself as he sighed. Coming upon the camp of his son, he saw the scene of mumble-jumble solitude that he'd experienced about thirty years ago when he'd "run away." Objects such as sacks, bread crusts, and other debris littered the area. On the ground, as if he were a part of it, lay Kevin. Rousing him to slight wakefulness, enough to get him to the car, he spoke in a sympathetic tone.

"Let's go home, son."

Whose Victory?
(part of the Scholastic Aptitude Test)

"T-sixty seconds and counting . . ." The voice is loud and Cape Kennedy is bustling with activity.

"T-thirty seconds and counting . . ." The voice begins to sound raspy. The situation is as tense to the millions of people watching as it is to the people at the Cape.

"T-ten, nine, eight, seven, six, five, four, three, two, one, ignition." With a mighty surge of power, the rocket takes off and the people see another billion-dollar craft find its way to the stars. Is this a step to becoming a winner or a loser? This paper will attempt to answer that question.

The launch is a type of victory—a victory in the field of aeronautics. Both the United States and Russia have had several of these victories. Russia has been successful with both the Sputnik and Cosmos series. The United States has met success with the Mercury and Gemini series and the most recent shot of Apollo.

Both sides, however, have problems which should be solved before such a large project is undertaken. The first common problem is the domestic programs of both countries which are suffering as a result of the space race.

In the United States, cities, morale, unity, and people need building. Poverty and mass disorders verging on anarchy need more attempts to determine their solution.

In Russia, a small minority has been demanding a voice in how their government is run. As the days go by, this minority could soon grow to be a majority.

What would the government do with its space program then? It would be forced to give it up and take instead the people's space program. In the domestic area, both sides are losers at this point.

The other common problem facing the two sides is the Vietnam conflict. It is only recently that both sides have begun to move toward each other. There can be no winner here because it's a question of existence and humanity is the only loser. The settlement of this problem has also taken a back seat to the space race.

The space race, like the Vietnam conflict, is one thing in which humanity either wins or loses. With each success, both sides could eventually create a system of interplanetary travel, which in turn would lead to increased knowledge of the worlds beyond us. With this knowledge, we could even find a way for people to survive on other planets.

The position we are in now, however, could increase our chances of self-destruction. Since the Russians and Americans differ on so many things now, these same differences could be present fifty years from now. The knowledge acquired about the universe by both sides could work against the human race. The establishment of interplanetary missile bases and eventual interplanetary war would create a losing situation with the result of self-destruction.

In concluding, there is only this to add. If the space race is used as a means to get arms, nuclear or otherwise, then and only then is the race a loss to both sides.

1970S

Committee to Reelect President Plans Takeover of U.S.

WASHINGTON—Watergate Inc., a two-thirds owned subsidiary of the Democratic Party, has become a wholly owned subsidiary of the Committee to Reelect the President under a break-in agreement signed, sealed, and delivered by the Committee.

The transaction is meant to comply with the 1972 consent decree between the Committee and ITT (In Troubled Times), requiring the United States to shed the two-party system before the November election.

The transaction is subject to the approval of President Nixon to the exclusion of the American people. Said transaction must also be approved by Jeb Magruder, John Mitchell, and H. R. Haldeman. The Committee to Reelect the President is expected to unanimously support the transaction.

Public holders and interested parties will receive unspecified amounts of monies for remaining silent in matters regarding the transaction. The Committee holds 205,000,000 shares, the public holds zero.

The Committee to Reelect the President will put up whatever financial base is needed and count on ITT for success. Payments for this transaction begin immediately after the Miami convention and bear a potential for impeachment.

Based on news article regarding TWA, a now-defunct airline, planning to take over Canteen, which at the time was two-thirds owned by IT&T. At the time I wrote this, I was working for Canteen as a janitor.

The Canteen Janitor

All right! In the name of the Puritan work ethic, I have a job. By some quirk, a friend of mine found a job for me where he works. To my astonishment, I find the place isn't a rowdy bar or a fragmented USO show, but a wholesale retail food outfit. I clean the place; I'm the Canteen janitor.

The building is a stucco structure with a yard full of machines on its left. Through the doorway, a counter confronts me—this, I'm told, is the front office. Vibrations of confusion, multiple errors, and a superficial aura of calm emanate from this area. My boss and his secretaries work here. What is inside this area is of higher importance than the outside appearance suggests. It's the nerve center of the business.

Through the second door, I find a huge kitchen. Here the cook and staff make as many as four hundred sandwiches a day. The kitchen is furnished with an array of refrigerators and a stove. Lingering aromas plus the sight of food effect a rumbling, raging tumult in my stomach. I am a janitor by night, a struggling student by day.

Through the third door, more food is visible, but most of it is of the munchy snack-time variety. Examples of candy, potato chips, pretzels, and sodas are in many areas. *Hang on, stomach!* I try to console myself by thinking that all those unopened cases and boxes are empty. My mental exercise doesn't alter the physical reality of being a hungry student.

Finally, I enter the machine yard. To my surprise, the yard is full of vending machines. At least fifty are immediately visible, others I'm certain are behind shop doors. What a bland existence! I imagine that they also have a certain amount of freedom. No longer do they endure the constant push and pull from unfeeling hands. I hurriedly hustle myself out of the machine yard and back to the warehouse.

I drag out my mop and broom. The people say nothing as they leave the hive of activity. I begin cleaning the detritus of the day. My stomach churning, toe tapping to internal rhythms, I begin with the front office. Upon my entry, I discover the boss has left me a message.

In easily read cursive handwriting, the memo reads, "Whatever the drivers leave in the fridge after their runs is yours if you can use it. I'd rather someone be fed than to waste food. Besides, the health department says there are time limits as to how long we can keep food."

Valentine hearts begin floating from every pore of my body. Food! Drivers? I look out the front door to see a fleet of twenty catering trucks. When I go back to the kitchen and open the fridge, I find a variety of nutritional and not-so-nutritional things. The pay may not be grand, but the perks are definitely nice. I celebrate my good fortune with a cup of coffee to which I've gleefully added chocolate milk. Friends can never be overrated.

A Contemporary Prometheus (apologies to Mary Shelley)

"When younger," said he, "I believed myself destined for some great enterprise. My feelings are profound but I possessed a coolness of judgment that fitted me for illustrious achievements. This sentiment of the worth of my nature supported me when others would have been oppressed, for I deemed it criminal to throw away in useless grief those talents that might be useful to my fellow creatures. When I reflected on the work I had completed . . . I could not rank myself with the herd of common projectors. But this thought . . . now serves only to plunge me lower in the dust. All my speculations and hopes are as nothing, and like the archangel who aspired to omnipotence, I am chained in an eternal hell. Even now I cannot recollect without passion my reveries while the work was incomplete. I trod heaven in my thoughts, now exulting in my powers, now burning with the idea of their effects. From my infancy I was imbued with high hopes and a lofty ambition; but how am I sunk! My friend, if you had known me as I once was, you would not recognize me in this state of degradation. Despondency rarely visited my heart; a high destiny seemed to bear me on, until I fell, never, never again to rise."

Has Dr. Victor Frankenstein been resurrected in the form of Richard M. Nixon? The dualism in both characters seems to affirm it. The creation of a monster by both men, Frankenstein and Nixon respectively, shouts for the comparison to be made. Finally, the tragedy of the doctor's attempt at immortality through a creation and the tragedy of Nixon's attempt at the same thing make the comparison apt.

Elegy to Mama Cass

This morning I am mourning the death of Cass Elliot
Who died choking on a ham sandwich,
An Epicurean delight; she excelled in the art of eating.
Now by her own hand, the maid, goodly stuffed,
Lies still with a smile beamin'
As the cortege intones strains of "California Dreamin'."
John, Michelle, Denny, all who earned a penny
With her on Creeque Alley now wish her bon voyage
And happiness to death's rally.

The Squeak Heard 'Round the World

Here we are at the world's oldest show-and-tell,

Animated fictional character animate man;

Visually the world is filled with fantasy pell-mell,

Enhancing the human race with antics of the cartoon clan.

A halt is called to the parade—the emcee clangs a bell,

Hundreds of people hush, straining to understand

Each word the elder mouse says if they can.

A message from the Selective Service? Hmm, something doesn't jell,

Reality has imposed on fantasy, this time it's the draft,

Though we say it can't happen because of Mickey's age.

Gall unmitigated is what they have, Mick, or maybe they're daft,

Uninformed of your fifty-two years of service sage;

You say it's time to say good-bye to all our company?

Say no, stand firm, your friends support you, Mr. M-O-U-S-E.

X

In Aix-en-Provence, I am reborn in each new day, minute,
second—

I am a pebble cast into a pond, producing concentric circles in
search of understanding.

Okay, I was the pebble, it was hot, and

I was tired of the outdoor student tour.

I unzipped my jumpsuit and clad in a Speedo,

Threw myself into the cool Seine, a drop of about ten feet.

I was taking a risk searching for that understanding!

Sinning, sunning, climbing up, and re-donning the jumpsuit,

As if nothing had happened, students smiling,

The tour continuing like nothing had happened.

Departing X

Arriving

Undulating

Rigid

Entire

Void

Odd

In

Royalty

Whisperings

Clouds whisper LIVE,
Winds whisper MOVE,
Rains whisper CLEAN,
Air whispers BREATHE,
Soul whispers GIVE.

Hydration

Instead of life being a regular flow
From a universal tap of thought,
It's a droplet from the tap,
Kersplooshing, forming ripples.
I'm a plant, where are my roots?

Love Leaf

A bee's affair with a flower does not equal mine with you,
Nor does a gentle rain shower convey the tenderness I give you
Freely, like the dew or the morning's mist.
How do I equate you or me singly or together?
Compassion and understanding intertwined
In a sparkle-sprinkled wilderness—
That's the equation, like the natural cycle,
Always living, always dying;
Like nature, whether sun or rain,
Soaking it up, always growing, you and I,
Rays of both glowing.
Beautiful catalysts to each other, sparking the moments,
Let's live them now, no time to turn,
Too little time, too much to learn.

Love Leaves

Murky clouds gather and envelop
Mountains in gossamer gloominess—
At the top, trees await the sky's tears.
A phosphorescent brook rolls on, tumbling rocks,
Depositing them to novel destinations, new beginnings.
I sit and contemplate with a hirsute pate,
An open-faced turkey san sitting on my plate.
Cleanse and clear the gloom, sky's and mine!
Decimate murkiness, so that I may see and not pine
For beauty I saw once, and now leave behind.

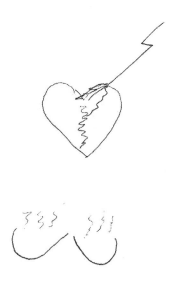

Phoenix

Hearts have been rended, awaiting airing,
Purification before mending
To continue beating, feeling, and loving.
For now, odorous putrefaction and
Love rotting with no possible bypass—
Let it be.
Adapt and change, to not do so would deny
Larvae, cocoon, and butterfly.
I will not wallow in the putrefied muck;
Rather let it go, find new love, give it wings, let it fly.

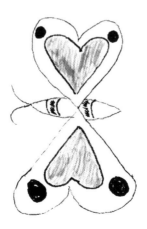

Joseph Kennedy

Machine Tender

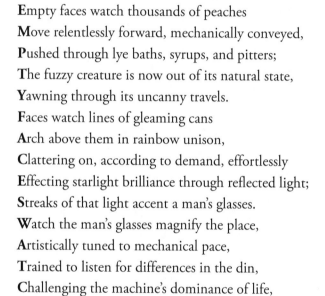

Empty faces watch thousands of peaches
Move relentlessly forward, mechanically conveyed,
Pushed through lye baths, syrups, and pitters;
The fuzzy creature is now out of its natural state,
Yawning through its uncanny travels.
Faces watch lines of gleaming cans
Arch above them in rainbow unison,
Clattering on, according to demand, effortlessly
Effecting starlight brilliance through reflected light;
Streaks of that light accent a man's glasses.
Watch the man's glasses magnify the place,
Artistically tuned to mechanical pace,
Trained to listen for differences in the din,
Challenging the machine's dominance of life,
Harnessed to its hypnotic efficiency.

Bluff? Raise? Call?

Fifty-two seconds welcome invasion, confusion—
Give the Iranians a full house;
Fifty-two minutes enter dissatisfaction, outrage!
Give the Americans a pair,
Ante up for the next hand, we've lost.
Fifty-two hours introduce tension, strain—
Give the Americans a five-card straight;
Fifty-two days bring happiness, disgust;
Give the Iranians a royal flush,
Ante up for the next hand, we've lost.
Shuffle into the game the Algerian jokers.
Fifty-six weeks extend vaunted wealth, gold bullion—
Give the Americans a banker's suit;
Fifty-six weeks show a fading illusion;
The Iranians fold,
Ante up for the next hand, it's a draw.
Sixty weeks establish change and chaos as the order of the day—
Give the Iranians a club suit;
Sixty weeks and a newly found courage
Give the Americans a suit of hearts;
Exit a beleaguered American team and raise the ante.
Sixty-three weeks and a new team
Give the Americans a pair of kings and the Algerian jokers;
Sixty-three weeks and a sense of waning power
Give the Iranians crazy eights;
Cash in the chips and pack up the deck,
We have won our fabulous fifty-two from Iran.

Dear Santa/Dear Joe

Dear Santa:

Why don't you come more than once a year? You help people think peaceful thoughts which they don't otherwise do. You really could delay wars if you wanted to. Before you come, why not stop by Heaven? It's on your way. Maybe with two of you working together, we could have both a happy and holy Christmas.

Also, please drop a match on certain department stores you judge to deserve. They commercialize Christmas to such an extent I believe the Star of Bethlehem is going on sale next week at Brack's for $1.98. If you could help people realize that Christmas trees are beautiful any time of the year, do you think that we would be more concerned with saving them rather than smothering them in concrete or asphalt?

Santa, you're probably decent, so maybe you can tell me why a society would find that cities and commercialism are so damn beautiful. I'm sure that you would agree that without commercialism, department stores, and cities to trump you up, you would not be. Since I find it hard to accept all of society's morals and customs, of which you are one, I find it difficult to accept your reality. You're welcome to prove me wrong, but you're going to have to talk, not b.s., me into thinking that society is always right, because there are no absolutes.

Dear Joe:

I've talked to "the Man" concerning you before when I was on my way down. We are definitely worried. I'm hoping it's the carbon monoxide you breathe but I fear it's more than that.

I'll tell you this—I'm not the one who has lied, nor am I the one who created the asphalt and concrete scars upon your land. I have not hated. I have not killed. I have not sinned against my brother. It is I who find it hard to accept the fact that someone like you—people—really exist. Do not blame me for man's wrongs. I exist only in love and good. If love and good do not exist, then there is no time for soft summer nights, frost on the windows, and snow on the hills in winter. There is no man, there is no woman. Even you do not exist, you only *are*! Evaluate and decide who and what you are. Please exist. I love life, do you?

Diamante

Rain

Wet, wild

Pelting, washing, nourishing,

Showers, thunder, lightning, cloudburst,

Canvassing, coloring, awe-inspiring,

Fine-tuned double

Rainbow

May Sharp

Birds warble in a harmonic key, brooks babble on endlessly,
Gliders soar upward peacefully, men move on pseudo-rhythmically,
Trees stretch to the sky gracefully, union is made merrily,
Friends share the mountains gleefully and life around them perceptibly,
Beethoven's notes envelop their day classically in the key of May.

River Camping

Strains of a melody are played double time
Fully representing sharps, flats, and rhythms;
Brook's syncopation, landscape's *fermata,* and
Constellation's slow motion *allegro*—
An unstoppable score full of dynamics *pianissimo* to *fortissimo*—
Bellissimo!

The–ing Trilogy

Advertising, cruising, rafting, tubing,
Out-boarding, in-boarding, sail boating,
Catamaraning, yachting, jet skiing;
Man above in pleasurable activity.
Eating, swimming, schooling, praying,
Staring, cavorting, bumping,
Surprising, surviving, dying;
Fish below man in habitat.
Flying, nesting, hunting, watching,
Fighting, mating, diving,
Flitting, befriending, searching,
Gulls above man above fish.

Tournament Judge

It's difficult being a mirror to someone you don't know;
Speechmakers try to paint a verbal canvas and I try judging their
colors' intensity.
It's easier to imbibe a rose's fragrance,
To be tickled by a pine needle,
To distinguish the mélange of voices in soccer,
Than it is to judge a person by what he or she says.

Mountainous Beauty

Three days in the mountains can work miracles;

Arboreal pyramids reach to touch an invisible point in the sky's vastness,

The pyramids support avian varieties of many colors with their own societies.

Beneath pyramids lie a lake, created by man for his enjoyment;

Let him not scale nature's pyramid further if he intends only to destroy what is not his.

If he can help nature add to her beauty, then let him try—

It is his domain to enhance and not to erase.

Night Walk

Everything is silent on the street that I walk,

Every step I take is muffled on concrete or asphalt block.

No crickets chirp, no frogs croak, even the air is still,

Yet the sky, with clouds, moves;

The moon, their hostess whispers, "We live—do not kill"

An auto roars by, the air reeks with gas, monoxide,

It poisons the sky at which I stare and exhale dioxide.

Solitude once more restored.

My body says it is too quiet, so it tries to make sound,

Mind over body, to body, "confound!"

All is so still, so cold—

Even a traffic signal, that mechanical monster of man,

Utters but clicks while the elements hold sway without any tricks.

Hostess moon rides her cloud men across Night's proffered sky;

On Earth is no equal, everything must die.

Full Employment

Winds burst the leaves from trees, blowing them crazily;
They spin them slowly to the ground, covering defined space
With a golden carpet in a late-autumn pattern.
The master carpet layers have given me a full yard of content—
It remains for rains to tack the carpet down.
Lightning illuminates the job for the wind to see,
The wind approves and whisks its workers forward haphazardly.

January Noon

Time-lapse clouds move too quickly
Foretelling a radical atmospheric change—
Deadly quiet ensues.
A sea-green cloud emerges and unleashes a sudden torrent of
water.
Rain-whipped window panes stream outside,
Fog up inside—a fluid reality seen.
Dark skies split in fractured thirds
As electrified threads weave violence.
Thunderous vibrations echo, illustrating
The gods playing four-square with a medicine ball,
Mimicking timpanist reality.

Fermez Les Portes

The staff is ambivalent,

Long friendships and professional umbilical ties are severed,

Yet each of them is free to pursue different tomorrows.

The students are happy to be out of enclosed space,

Released into summertime pace.

One last hug from a child to his elder friend,

Then memories whirl through the halls, flood the classrooms,

Attempting to find a person to encircle,

To breathe an idea of what this place was.

This school is closed, a victim of financial woe,

But stand in the hall, feel the wind blow—

Is everyone really gone?

The Bearded and the Beardless

The smell of barbecue was in the air
As the two tennis stars appeared on the court;
Amid blaring rock and roll and a child's stare,
The games began—racquets often swung at air
Where eyes had been certain something was there.
Beardless swung once, then in a chasing pirouette, swung again.
In the gallery, the child laughs;
Bearded man fell while reaching for a shot—
His opponent, concerned, asked if he was all right.
Bearded man led the set five games to two—
The opponent summoned the courage to fight back;
Vicious volleys, lazy lobs, sizzling serves,
Alley shots, net shots, line shots, tied the set at five games each.
In the gallery, the child applauds.
Bearded and Beardless rolled and ran until Beardless won—
He shook hands with his wheel-chaired opponent
As the child looked on in wonderment.

Christmas Freeze-Frame

'Tis the season of momentum,
Fa la la la la la la la la;
Open greetings, Yuletide cheer,
Fa la la la la la la la la;
Madhouse shopping, humanity hoofing,
Fa la la la la la la la la;
Brightness and skies that are crystal clear,
Fa la la la la la la la la.

Friends, acquaintances and new faces,
Fa la la la la la la la la;
Blitzing, darting, flashing, sparkling,
Fa la la la la la la la la;
A day bedazzled with Christmas comets,
Fa la la la la la la la la;
Movements take their toll and now I rest,
Fa la la la la la la la la.
Chatting to friends about our bargains,
Fa la la la la la la la la;
Gazing into tides of humanity,
Fa la la la la la la la la;
Rolling, overtaking, cresting each other,
Fa la la la la la la la la;
Living, breathing waves of collective pulses,
Fa la la la la la la la la.

Who's the Photographer?

A mountain thundershower has trapped my camera and me beneath a tree;

Mild moisture moves to a calypso beat as mists give the air freshness;

Sun enters the picture turning the rain transparent;

Photographs continue quickly clicking until a loud boom rends the air!

Rain, though light, is steady, my camera and I are ready,

But not for another boom—is someone else taking a shot?

The lens cap goes on, my camera surrenders,

The rain now is fast and hard, my tree surrenders as guard.

Boom! Am I trying to outrun a bombardier?

Rain falls so hard it forms rivulets from splatters,

Calypso beat gives way to cannon roar as the photographer snaps some more.

A blinding flash of lightning, then thunder,

Raindrops become rain rocks—

Does the sky use a tripod?

In minutes, transformations from blue to gray

To sprinkle to downpour to ice;

Nature's photographer too is capturing life

But her shutter release should be checked.

Three Corners

It rains yet I'm not wet—how bizarre—
I round the corner of the building
And meet with wet fury a nearly horizontal sheet of water;
On looking up into lights, a rolling, cascading wet ball—
Is there a game called wet bowling? If so, where are the pins?
Or someone is unrolling a large carpet with a bit of water in it.
I round another corner and become a pin—
Liquid rat-a-tats pepper my back,
Pushing water beneath my feet,
Making me want to play "Jump the Creek."
Muddy yuck flows into the stream at a confluence,
Perhaps, nature is polluting herself.
I round one more corner and become stream-faced,
Cavorting onward, laughing;
Not even water laps can bring me down,
I'm wet and, for now, happy about it.

The Big Bear

The Big Bear is on the loose once more,
Bar your windows, lock your door;
He seeks food for an already-full tummy,
He is after more, my, were they yummy;
From nation to nation he thinks he can go,
Never sick, always quick to please an overzealous ego.
He has taken democracy and crumbled it to bits
In countries where it was not strong;
All this to satisfy himself and put them where he thinks they belong.
From liberty and freedom he shrinks away,
It's not that he is shy, you know;
It's another reason—the fear that he might die that day
And leave the seeds he was supposed to sow,
To grow into one strong lie.
When the warnings and everything else have failed,
His death he doesn't need to worry over.
On a small country the bear is let loose
To accomplish his task and to the people he'll roar;
The big bear's reasoning and truths are confused,
Facts he distorts, stories he reverses, leading people astray.
You know what happens if they find the truth?
Down on your knees, Big One, and pray.
Your taming and destruction will come one day
Not from bomb, missile, or gun,
But from people you lead who will see their mistake
In putting up with you, you big bare fake.

Unity

From television, magazine, radio, press, and book,
You have been able to find that this word provokes thoughts in your head;
What you fail to understand about this word is that its ring is dead,
Its tacit absence has made the world for unity look.
Its departure has filled leaders and people alike with much fear,
Is it any wonder as of its definition and use, there's not much to hear?
Are people afraid of its measure, what is there to dread?
Has its absence split people or taken something near?
With this word which helps man's chorus and is five letters long,
The world can harmonize, acting as one.
Its leaders, its instruments, can solve other discords right or wrong,
And the far-reaching effect, its *fermata*, on people will not be undone.
The word itself could inspire simple song—
Unity—when all things form perfection and a cause sounds its gong.

Smile Eagle

"**S**" added to laughter changes its tone from simple mirth to total shock,

And strikes stupidly, unconcernedly at all life *avec ou sans bon*;

"**M**" added to end repairs a break done to bone or person,

And consoles, carefully connecting the triad to help them respond;

"**I**" added to deal transforms a packaged anything to definition,

And enlarges a dream, enveloping it in magnified form;

"**L**" added to bend alters a large group of dissonant players

Into a harmonic balance of melody and accompaniment that encases aural sense;

"**E**" added to SMIL brings light. glee, joy,

Mirth, beauty, loving, caring,

And hoping the end is not the button of an atomic toy.

Hit-and-Run Rain

Indoors, a class of boredom,

Outdoors, clouds wait;

Suddenly, eaves dripping, rivulets running, people scurrying—

Suddenly, it's raining.

Outdoors, sunshine and steam,

Indoors, clouds of anxiety;

Suddenly, jaws flapping, eyes scanning, brains remembering—

Suddenly, it's test time—

Gone at a glance, hit-and-run rain.

Doo-Dad Rain

Stale, rarefied air from a square classroom;
Help! Escape! I need change,
The door is open, go now.
Silent students bustle on to their next classes
While I am caressed by a fresh and cool dampness;
It's a cleaner, more vibrant air that allows
My sludgy walk to become a relaxed gait.
Light rain invisible on concrete
Is sensed on my tongue, hair, and skin;
The sky is adorning me with diamonds.
Doo-dad rain touches an ethnic memory
Of verdant pastures, ivy-covered cottages,
And people singing lilting melodies;
Doo-dad rain brings memories of long ago
And visions of different presents—
It tells of lovelier, livelier airs that continue the bloom of a child.

Shadows

When the time comes to decide
Who starts my day, me or my clone,
What would keep me from saying neither?
I know that my twin would be precise,
Exacting my every attitude, every idiosyncrasy;
I think that's why I wouldn't trust him,
He's too efficient, too perfect;
How could I accept my own reproduction?
I think that's how I would lose me;
Besides, a character I know goes where I go—
It's always natural and loyal, always my shadow.

Good Ol' Tom

Good Ol' Tom was born one day
With one mark agin him, 'twas black, they say;
Otherwise normal, but for that one mark,
Tom's mind, like Tom, became quite dark.
In a decrepit ol' slum, he came to be,
A black ol' man, a worthless decree;
Rats his best friends and whites his foe,
All helped stanch intellectual flow.

Then one day, the militant view
Cooked Ol' Tom in a riotous stew;
He didn't know what the mixture was
But got included anyway and so did his cause.
The stew bubbled, boiled some say,
And took a few people as it flowed its way.
Get it off the stove! The cry came late,
As the mix boiled over, hot with hate;
The fires flared, the windows broke,
Clubs found their marks with many swift strokes.
People screamed their surrender, Ol' Tom was one,
Too bad for him, one shot, he's done;

On the ground he laid, a quiet frame,
Waiting for treatment that never came.
Fifteen died with him that night
In a street turned graveyard, a tourist's sight;
By next morn, the city was quiet,
No one was sure if this ended the riot.

Only fifteen corpses did officials see,
Ol' Tom was missing, where could he be?
Good Ol' Tom was found soon enough,
Beaten by a white man who stood tall and tough.
"I only tried to stop him," his answer came,
"From damaging my home, now I think he's lame."
The white man was tried the very next day,
For first-degree murder he was to pay;
His chamber ready, gas its décor,
The man stepped in and was heard from no more.

As for Ol' Tom, he now lies at rest,
Relieved of life's tensions, relieved of life's tests;
With fire on his left and ignorance on the right,
Tom lies buried within plain sight.
Ignorance and fire have been buried with one,
With millions of others, the harm's not done;
To keep it away, we only need a solution—
Why not go color-blind?

Sally Christian

Tickled under the chin caressingly by lady fingers,
Surrounded by a harmonic world carefully
With a musician's dexterity, I am transfixed—
I am a porcelain miniature in giant hands.
Stimulated senses stirred gently by a postured pianist,
Artfully encased in velvet skin;
By a musical tailor I have been fitted,
A rich emperor with noteworthy clothes.
Influenced by Spanish suggestively with an electric air,
Ringed with matadors and guitarists,
Playfully by the playmaker arranged,
So that I join the play that the hands make.

Mankind

Old man on bicycle meets young man on disabled moped;

Friendly glances invite conversation of the open kind,

Tasty tidbits of ribald stories from his youth touch mine,

Enabling me to see a boy in this man's smiling eyes

Naturally, as if there were no sense of "older."

I listen, laugh, cry, wink, and arch my eyebrows in mock surprise,

Ceasing only when he asks why I am so quiet and nice;

Am I quiet? Our reflections of each other

Recount stories of his past and my future, and the wonder

Evident in both underscores how little time we have now.

Lunar Eclipse

"Lights Out" signals a darkening orb surrounded by a petticoat of stars,

Moon's face has gone from cream to copper;

Night noises have ceased except for an owl querying "Who?"

And the guttural displeasure of a mountain lion—

My awareness is increased, listening for the slightest disturbance;

My time exposure is finished and before I change the camera's position,

I will build my campfire higher to the absentee moon.

Fog Samurai

Fog shrouds the road and lowers as we travel higher—

The car is a cocoon of warmth against the enveloping, stealthy mist

That finally blinds the viewer to what's ahead,

Fog is the impersonal, pesky time machine.

Suddenly, brightness and hope in a patch of blue,

Poof! Fog vanishes;

Ahead lay houses, mountains, and a clear sky,

Behind me, a swirling array of dew-drop knives.

Dream Sequences

Awaking under a bowl of stars, the moon bathing the landscape;

Awaking under a coastal sun, char-broiled, the Pacific lapping a few feet away;

Swimming underwater, leaving anchored boats, pelicans,

And seals bobbing to the tune "Celebration."

Conversing with ladies who attract butterflies and comment on my nudity;

Hiking bluff trails, stumbling on or across occasional wildlife;

Listening to percussive African rhythms in a sheltered cove;

Envisaging miles of marine food chain affected by offshore oil drilling;

Dissipating fog before an authoritarian seer;

Sleeping, dreaming, and waking are all enjoyable sequences.

Hello, Agatha Christie

Misting morning moisture moves at a snail's pace through the fog-lidded valley;

Fields of vision become obscure fields of soup, shrouded in a mysterious envelope.

"Miss Christie, what or who, was or is, there?"

Deafening silence in the fog world below as a sun sneers from above.

Working at Nothing

I reported to work at my usual time, usual for me, but for no other segment of humanity. Most people were home by 12:30 a.m., but for seven hundred people, including myself, it was only a beginning. Like so many beginnings, the endings couldn't be foretold. The JST towers were foreboding, seven stories of blank concrete outside, seven stories of blank faces inside. Most of the jobs were of a maintenance nature. As fast as the state could erect the slabs, there were people to tend to them. Janitorial work was the rule and tonight janitors were being paid overtime since a convention was coming the next day. One had to be certain all floors were antiseptically clean, since no one was sure how many floors would be used.

This evening was the end of my first week at JST and my excitement over this ending probably had something to do with it being payday. Excitement was rare the entire week because most people were either being trained to do their jobs or were attempting to apply that training to the work they were doing. Sometimes the two were related; more often, they weren't.

After walking the half mile from the parking lot, I checked in with security. Their job was to certify that I was who I said I was. After agreeing that the only change I had made was the growth of sideburns, I was allowed passage to my floor, the fourth. The music inside the building was mesmerizing, too heavily orchestrated, and monotonous. Efforts at obtaining a tape with modulation had failed. So we adapted the B-flat tape to fit. Through a series of dubs and overdubs, the instruments managed to sound like they attained different notes. Strings strung along in D, low brass blatted in B-flat, flutes fluttered an F, and trumpets blared B-flat above the staff.

I was on the second floor now after saying hello to a guard I had never seen before on the first floor. This floor contained the sixty people who maintained the electrical systems. Each sat at a console that kept watch on everything from clocks to toilets. Numerous toilet outages had been reported four days ago. Instead of flushing, the things were uplifting the loads. None of the electricians, twenty of whom were on this floor, could explain the sudden reversal.

Until tonight, I had not known what functions were on the first floor. The guard I encountered answered my question by saying that the hundred guards hired by JST were headquartered there.

The third floor contained dusters, washers, moppers, dryers, and shiners. The floor was tended by these five people along with three backup teams consisting of five people each. Their job was to tend the machines that did most of their job for them. By color-coding a series of jobs, each person could direct the machines along with the careful guidance of the computer. More than once, a new worker had used an obsolete color code with results ranging from a batch of cookies made from the batched newsprint of the day to an uncoded batch of forms that had the main computer completely befuddled.

After seeing another guard I didn't know, I entered my floor. There was nothing strange about seeing guards I didn't know since there were so many. My floor had the dubious task of opening the night's mail. Due to variations in volume, there were variations in manpower. Tonight there were one hundred people, the entire crew, all opening letters, looking for something exciting. Last night, we had found some pornography and work ceased while the pictures were passed around. As a result, some of the crew began to touch each other. The supervisors allowed this for fifteen minutes, but put a stop to it before matters got out of hand. There were one hundred thousand pieces of mail to read, forms to fill out, and questions and summaries to be sent to the fifth floor.

Tonight I was to take the summaries. At 6:00 a.m., I walked the stairs to the fifth floor since the people mover was out of order. I passed another guard I didn't recognize. *Three for the night, it must be a complete overhaul,* I thought. Stepping through the door to the fifth floor, I abruptly halted. A small fire from a cigarette had started, but that was the only sign of life in the room. Ordinarily there were one hundred forty-five people working furiously at sorting questions, picking the summaries apart for important items. Where was everybody? The only guess I had was that there had been a security check.

On the sixth and seventh floors of the tower, the guards were all women. The tower employed some two hundred security people, but only thirty guarded the top two floors. The reasoning was that if the massive forces on the first floor didn't clear you, you must've looked secure. A security check was also here, but with thirty guards the check was minimal and useless. The sixth floor was the depository for outgoing mail. It was here that the summaries were checked before being stuffed into envelopes, stamped, and sent out. One hundred and seventy people worked here, having to be instructed that since they were civil employees, they should attempt civility with each other. I told one of the guards about the cigarette fire burning on the fifth floor, and then left.

At precisely the moment I left, an evacuation alarm sounded. Directors, most of whom were on the seventh floor, loved to see employees jostle for their lives. One never knew how many floors were being evacuated; one just moved as ordered. This time, we were being shuffled to the shelters between the sixth and seventh floors. The inter-floor shelters led directly to heliports where quick escape was mandatory to sustain life in time of emergency. Usually we would've been flown to "Le Cadran Suspendu," where we would stay varying lengths of time until safety could be guaranteed.

Instead, we were being hastily led to the seventh floor, the director's floor. Under no circumstances were we to be on this floor. No one within JST had the authority to grant access to this floor of vaults. The money, all of it in government bonds, was kept here. Upon entering this floor, we first saw our guards take off latex masks to expose faces no one knew. The ninety-five directors were all tied together resembling a sunburst due to their bright orange and yellow uniforms. The guards kept them moving in a counter-clockwise direction and the supervisors were stumbling over each other. The guards calmly explained that the directors were eventually going to generate enough heat to burn down the building and that we all would die in the resulting inferno. To illustrate how this was to happen, one of the guards turned the thermostat to fifty degrees Fahrenheit, and let us watch as the directors quickened their paces to keep warm. Each of them was oblivious to the fact that the generators were storing their heat.

People were beginning to protest. As an example of what could happen should there be wide scale fighting, the guards took twenty-five of the staff to a rendezvous with the steam chamber. They ceased to be at a temperature of 412 degrees. The rest of us were trying to figure out alternatives to this pressure-cooker scenario. The monitors were aglow with what was happening on other floors. The first and second were empty, the third was being pierced with laser beams. Some of the people were scrambling from fires; others were being engulfed by them. Helipads and bicyclocopters were scattered over the early morning sky. The nearest aid was sixty kilometers from here at "Le Cadran Suspendu."

It was nearly sunrise and at 8:00 a.m., a new shift would be here viewing empty rooms, always being absently present at their jobs. No one would suspect a thing. We were being steamed at the rate of twenty-five every thirty minutes. Since 2:30 a.m., one hundred and twenty-five had been executed, forty-five remained. Twenty-five were being corralled now. Sensing the finale, I turned and yelled, "Let's go!"

We ran to the exit but got no further. The guards lined us up with hands on pipes then turned the steam up. Forty-five piercing shrieks broke every light bulb in the immediate vicinity and triggered the guards to flip the generator switches. The directors continued directing and the machine was exuding intense heat. Things began to melt. One of the guards came up to me, incensed by my shrieks. I pulled at his face only to find that it was real, not latex. He told me to forget about putting the fire out and help get people out of the building. My sense of heroism gone, I told him each person could find his own way out.

He then said, "Several people have wanted something exciting to happen on their shifts. Collective telepathy readings show that if something exciting happens, then the drabness factor of their jobs is reduced. After a titillating incident, their wits are honed to their former sharpness and they are again civil to each other."

"But don't they want more incidents then?" I ventured curiously.

"No, because after the experience, each person will have his or her own version of what happened. In this way, pieces of the action will be remembered, but not the entire incident. After all, we're only human. The pieces that are remembered will be exchanged for so long that only a thread of truth will remain. When they are bored with the truth, they will then think past the obvious truths of their situations to underlying truths. Since all else is conjecture, this process will go on indefinitely. The experience should satisfy them for at least sixty working days."

"What about the deaths?" I asked tentatively.

"By Aquarius' flow, no! They didn't die; they underwent a recycling process that purified them of boredom. The remaining purified molecules were then collected and through a system of skin coding, were reassembled. When they return to their jobs tomorrow night, They will know only that they have been through something together. Our main goal in life and death is to bring people together. The rest is illusion."

With that last comment, guard number four, our president, turned and walked away. I awaited the reconstruction, watching number four fly in his bicyclocopter toward "Le Cadran Suspendu."

Ceremonial Gathering

Unacquainted people sit together on a grassy knoll staring at grave
markers
While a breeze breathes life into death's face;
We try to accept a death of one of our own—
Every man and woman does it.
The preacher mumbles "Praise God"
And asserts that the dead man has gone to a better place—
If death is its own reward, then why is there life?
People lived, loved, needed, and knew the dead man,
Who are his friends now?
We weep over the life and death conflict,
Oddly unhappy with the former and doomed to the latter.

Feed and Forget

Relatives, friends, countrymen,

Drop the tragic mask and put on the other;

Eat, drink, greet, and speak of accomplishments,

Of children, status, love, experiences,

For only the living know and appreciate them—the dead don't

care.

Good-bye

A telephone call reports my grandfather's death—

We refuse to believe and,

Unsettled, we leave to be with other relatives.

The gasoline station brings happiness and a wedding caravan!

We refuse to believe and,

Confused, we leave to be with less happy people.

The call brings loss,

I refuse to believe—

Undaunted I leave and scream angrily,

"I never got my Jeep ride!"

Collision

REM deep sleep interrupted by a drunken wild man;
A fight ensues and I fight to kill.
Hair torn, knees rug-burned, egos bent,
Survival is the thing.
Wild man has no idea of his intrusion into personal space;
He fights against a concept, human rights,
Taking his misunderstandings and violently projecting them
On the very people he might otherwise love;
Hate is the thing.
Shattered glass door, adrenalin-wired and sore,
Two grapplers on the floor;
Shouts of "faggot" and "kill the whore!"
Intolerance is the thing.
The attacker ceases the attack,
Finger and strangle marks pearl his neck;
Of the two, which is fairer,
Bruised openness or strangled ignorance?
Tolerance is the thing.

Brite Clearing

Each steep step I take brings me nearer to a clearing I remember
from childhood;
I don't move as quickly now,
There is time to study animal habits, habitats, and breathe deeply
The crystalline air.
Under powder blue skies, I hear pines moan, birds' cacophony, and
human laughter,
All layered upon a sweeping panorama of forest, mountain, valley.
In the clearing, ceremonial memories dance,
Clothing casually flung for a sunshine celebration.
A hawk's shadow visits my body, celebration short-lived;
Dressing hastily, sensing danger, feet carry me quickly.
Crunching twigs, a long object with low, cold eyes;
Pounding pulse, increasing footfalls, descant descent,
At the bottom of the hill, the hawk sits on a fencepost staring in the
direction I came.
I turn to see a long and low object skulking away and,
Terror-stricken, my hands cup cold water onto my face.

Afterthought

Strange lady gives me a receipt for a la carte food;
I slowly sit down and wonder,
What if I want a refund after I've eaten it all?
Do I give the food back or will the receipt suffice?

Love Shared

So many things to say when love is in the air,
To say them all subtracts from its intensity;
Nature wishes us well even though our inner natures are unseen—
We are compatible folks.
To become one would insult our uniqueness;
Love is important to us both, we crave it.
Love is not all we have in common;
As our lives progress, love is one item in the kit.
Distance between us will never matter,
For when we see each other again,
We'll be at the party of the Mad Hatter.

Jackpot at Three

Solitary pulls of the handle bring symbols of favor—three cherries;
Astonishments appear as measured money rains into the pan—JACKPOT!

Nearby, a reeking stench of sweat and alcohol,

Clad in a decrepit plaid suit coat, gabardine trousers,

Tennis shoes, an Emmett Kelly hat, an eccentric melancholy.

"Can I touch it?" A small ventriloquist voice;

"Go ahead," I'm rich;

Childhood disbelief, a bum's wry grin.

"I need breakfast."

"What happened to 'gotta dime for coffee, mister?'"

"Times are changin'. No one has just coffee for breakfast. It ain't good nutrition. I gotta be fit."

"Okay. Here. One silver dollar." How magnanimous, I think.

"Have a good day."

Off he wanders, curious creature, probably more off than on;

I collect my winnings unaware of the fashionable lady behind me,

Struck across the face by the difference in "have" and "have not."

Up, Up, and Away

Predawn light and a half moon await the signal of sunrise;
People run with two skinny sheets of lengthening nylon,
Two baskets sit alone. Two fans start filling two throats—
We two riders wait entranced.
Skinny nylon sheets begin to assume a shape;
Air bubbles traverse through them, rapidly forming mini zeppelins.
Quick-paced evolution continues as the shape grows,
Dwarfing us two riders;
Flames flicker, heating the air inside this suddenly winged peacock—
There are sendoffs, waves, we two wish the first riders farewell.
The voyage beckons us next, into the gondola we climb
With childlike excitement, awe, and wonder;
Gently we rise, peppering the navigator with questions.
Casting a glance down, we're a thousand feet above the ground
Quickly, effortlessly, lightly, no sensation of rising but for popping ears.
The sky is wide and winds are capricious
As we adapt to the thinner air.
Feelings of unease are checked by an endless sense of curiosity;
We climb to fifteen hundred feet, sharing space with a glider;
Doubling our altitude, we view the Kern River below,
As breathtaking in enlarged version from above as it is

Joseph Kennedy

Breathtaking in its miniature one on the ground.
The balloon began as a miniature on the ground too,
Yet grew to its statuesque height of seven stories—
In the sky's vastness, it still appears miniature!
Much too soon, it's time for descent;
Smoothly, imperceptibly we fall from the sky,
Encountering confused jackrabbits running amok
As the shadow covers them momentarily.
The gondola bounces once on the ground,
The second bounce is harder and knocks us around,
The third bounce we land but the wind is playing for keeps.
I give the rope a strong pull;
I'm no match for the wind that tilts us, willing us back up.
The chase vehicle is visible, wending its way to us
The long way, having to detour around an oil sump—
We are balls in a pinball game; the wind is the Pinball Wizard.
We are targets acquired now by the chase vehicle,
Safely we've landed, and have a champagne toast;
I toast my partner and navigator, then holler,
"Santé" to the sky as I lift my glass.
The balloon was bubbly full, now my belly balloon is.

1980S

Bicentennial Valentine

Effortlessly living, idly potentializing, life's pastels kaleid;
The Younger, the Elder, she petulant, he crotchety, span the ages;
We shorten distance in a mechanical bubble as we lengthen the pine's whine.
Arrival at needed point, bubble bursts, birds converse then move on;
The sun shines on inanimates as lizards beneath scrabble for lunch in the junkyard;
Mirror is found, purchase is made,
The sun publicly fades, privately asking return
As winter breezes remand the air with chilly fingers;
Imperceptible closures lock in the air's heaviness.
Upon leaving, a look at alley cats celebrating mediocrity—
One smiles its greetings over freshly finished tantalizing bird.

Suddenly, star-design cracks, rapidly tossed bodies, the Younger inside, the Elder outside!
Void, infinity, and eternity;
I hear my name and cannot respond to my younger sister as she watches me dissociate;
Slow turn of head, life undecidedly flitting,
Red flows over black, life over asphalt.
Moans **O**ccur **R**ushing **T**hinly,
As charged blackness surrounds my life rose.

Medicinal salts, ambulance voices bring brief awareness;
"Which hospital?" he asks a dissolving entity,
I reply and sink into the abyss.
Bright and stark lighting, people running, life vacillating,
I'm here. Where? All my body seems pulled into my head.
How could life's respecter try to end his?
Tears.
"How did it happen?" an officer asks a death-white mime;
I try to rise from the gurney to get something for lunch, where am I?
Loud voice: "You never let a patient with a head injury get up and walk!"
Thanks, Mom, I discover later.
Hunger and death are lurking outside in the corridor
As doctors patch and nurses attend a battered shell;
Glass splinters removed from head mirror
Reflections of spilled intelligence filling visual space.
Tears stream burning open flesh,
Memory is faulty while trying to store feelings and experiences;
Electric-blue pallor visits, stays on reflexes turned to ice;
The needle nourishes, injects stimulus.

Death and I meet,
My hand is taken by a silhouetted figure in a parson's hat;
We walk slowly to a walled grotto, where a singular brightness emanates;
Odd, there's an opening just large enough for a person to walk through—
I feel no fear, only contentment, where am I?
A voice, gentle and soothing says,
"You are not ready for this and this is not ready for you."
Barely alive, barely relating, barely me,

Doctors console a halted personality.
My head is shaved to remove glass shards—
Assassins! Please, no more pain! No more feeling!
Tears.
Darkness, then sitting erect, staring blankly;
Another injection, the needle and I are becoming friends.
Years seem to pass unheard, unseen—
Death departs, taking the shadow and returning mine;
I awake feeling weak as we roll somewhere else,
Through a hallway of people rushing and preparing;
There is an abrupt halt as a cold x-ray table contacts me.
Bombardment of light, then I'm fetal;
My shadow notes my fears and laughs
As hunger and sadness are in the ring trading jabs.
A man with a star, I see you. Why? How? Explain.
He doesn't exist. Illogical.
Non-recognition of loved ones causes them grief;
Mother, father, sister, brother, aunt, uncle,
Only my mind reaches out, can you hear me?
Incessant gurney rolling upsets a drawn stomach
While fatigue causes images to wax out of focus.
An antiseptic room I share with a frightened child
Mirrors my own child's fright;
Her anguished screams cause me to consider murder;
A nurse calms the little girl then wheels her away,
I wish her well.
Spoon-fed nutrition, stomach rebellion, and the nurse retreats,
Returning with the needle and now I lay me down, down, down;
People talking, shadow reappearing, am I ready?
There is nothing but stillness and tranquility.
Epochs of my life play in musical sixty-fourths,
Space out of fluid time,
Rhapsodic rhythms, simple symphonies, mental orchestras.
"Your name? Hello in there," a male voice says,

Looking into my bloodshot eye, dim light source moving.
Drug-induced brain game, there's no one there,
This has happened before.
To the other eye, audio and visual are on the same team again;
Orbs, though not completely open, view a living, breathing being—
I am no longer my own mystery guest.
"M—my name?" "I am J-J-Joe! Joe! I am here."
Orbs open, his face is in my face,
"What day is it?" he asks. I don't know—that one's too tough.
He says, "February 14, 1976."
Tears.
Telepathic messages outgoing, are they received?
Doctor, I am unable to embrace you, I do, though.
Did I say it? Did he get it? Did I even think it?
He gives me a friendly touch in an unhurt spot,
He loves you, Doc.

Tell Me Why

All we are asking is give peace a chance:
We will continue to ask, mindful of the alternative;
Come together, John and Yoko, blended honesties;
Imagine no war, no mind games, a lovely Norwegian Wood.

Beaming parents and a beautiful boy exchange caresses, touches, tickles.
Mr. Kite, a Nowhere Man, believes happiness is a warm gun.

John Lennon is shot and Sean is a fatherless son;
For your benefit, Mr. Kite, Eleanor Rigby
Picks up a face that she keeps in a jar by the door.
Nowhere Man, please listen, you don't know what you're missin',
You erased a human life;
Why? Who is it for?

Four-Dollar Employment

One—you could have more,
One requirement met will give you more.
Two—What type of work could I do to have money enough
To keep me from worrying about having enough?
Three—How do I match my likes knowing
Three are not monetarily rewarding?
Four—list opportunities, needs, wants, decisions, indecisions,
For four dollars still await a community quorum.

Vacancy

"Look, it has two bedrooms," "I wonder who lives up there?"

"Me, may I know you?"

"Landlord says it's an older man."

"Old? Let's just say continuously expanding."

"He's quiet and we won't know he's there." "Landlord says he's almost invisible."

"Wow, of all the names I've been called, invisible wasn't one."

"No one wants him, he's waited too long."

"Ah, but I'm still alive and needed."

I would like to be acquainted with you, possible neighbor;

With this attitude, however,

The best thing to do is close the door and let the vacancy remain,

And be invisible only to those who will not see.

Keening Christmas

A middle-aged couple, she with blond hair and in tears,

He with brown hair and sobbing,

Pack their belongings, halting at a corner

That contains many Christmas gifts given to them over the years.

Lavender soaps are in front of them,

She wails over her losses in life,

He sings in a booming baritone over his.

Through their tears and shared losses, they forge strength,

Hanging ornaments in the corner and dancing with their unified
sorrows;

Oblivious to them, a younger gentleman, alone,

Is moving new things into the loft above,

Intent, alone, on a solo goal, to get it done and be moved in—

The magic of Christmas unwraps itself instead,

On the evening of the summer solstice.

Narcissus Becomes Adonis

The harsh dawn of a hot morning reveals a mirror-lined room
Filled with men lifting, preening, improving themselves;
To my right a man yells, grunts, and groans with his exercise
While to the left another finishes hurriedly,
A Mad Hatter in gym trunks and tank top.
Yet another one struggles valiantly, mutters obscenities, and quits.
Observation grants me solace—
I will look and feel better than they, refreshed and sore
simultaneously.
Listen to the body and make faces in that mirror;
Wonder if anyone gets out of it alive,
And seriously question the "Let's all look thin" jive.

1990S

The Mask

The mask, in its roughest state, represents the teaching field in general. In all phases, from research to planning, to the presentation in front of the audience, it's rarely smooth. There are times when it appears to be smooth, but those moments are highly illusory. For instance, research and planning of a lesson or activity may have gone superbly, yet the actual presentation, because of a myriad of unforeseen variables, falls flat on its face.

The striped shirt on the forehead represents the teacher's role as referee, whether in the classroom, or outside of it. The five globes above that shirt represent the teacher as he/she attempts to juggle many things at the same time. The blue symbol represents boys, the pink one girls. Often the referee is solving or pointing to the solution of a problem between a boy and a girl or groups of boys and girls, boys and boys, or girls and girls.

The glasses appear on the face to portray the early need for visual assistance that many teachers require because of the sheer volume of paperwork associated with their jobs. They also illustrate the teacher's role as manager of a small city, the classroom, and as a liaison to that city's mayor, the principal. The light bulb stands for the inventor role in teaching and the fact that some inventions will succeed and some won't.

The magnifying glass on the left side of the face is there to illustrate the role of detective in teaching. It is meant to symbolize the constant search for truth in the daily dealing between teacher and student(s). The pair of wings suggests the role of nurturer and protector, how teachers take their students under their wings for a limited time and then set them free, hoping they will soar.

The star appears on the face to emphasize the teacher's role as enforcer of classroom rules, playground rules, school rules, etc. The magician's hat represents the many times we are expected to be flexible, often at the last moment, no matter what the original plan is or was. The red cross signifies the roles of counselor, medic, nurse, emergency friend, and so on. The graphic at the bottom right is meant to be an island; each teacher is one—almost; that is why the water does not completely encircle the land.

Finally, the chain of comedy/tragedy masks illustrates the role of the teacher as an actor/actress. There are many facets to that role, not the least of which is the ability to play a variety of roles on a daily basis and change them at the drop of a hat (the magician's), if needed. It is placed across the lips to show that the field is full of both comedy and tragedy and that it may not be wise for a teacher to make a verbal response to everything.

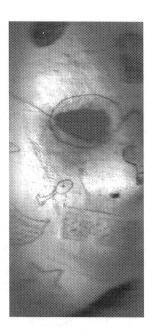

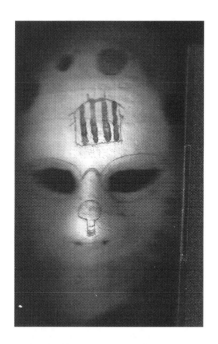

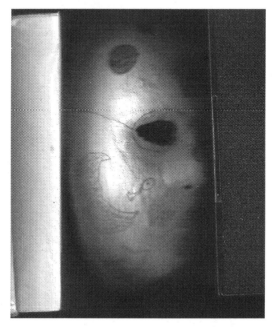

2000S

Tag

Sunrise brings oppressive, intolerable, moist heat
Locked in by a leaden cloud-laden sky,
Bringing to mind molds, mosses, rare fungi.
Drops of light poison spastically fall, not forming
Puddles or rivulets—they form nothing.
Ah, but sunset orange bids adieu to the blue
And tints clouds softly with pinks, purples, and starkly etched whites;
Twilight enters on its rickshaw as the sun beats a retreat on its chariot,
Awaiting the next day's chase.

Poignant Bridge

Two cards, two friends, two bridges—
One a travelling sixtyish naturalist,
Curious about cultures, people, places;
One a grateful eighteenish student,
Curious about people, writing, events,
Both abridged to this fiftyish gent—
One bridge to two, two bridges to one;
Curious about all, fortunate to build bridges of interest,
He grateful for bridges built to him and
The resulting polyphonic interests.

Abutments

Bright and beautiful sunshine, piled with cotton-ball cumulus,
Tinged purple, abut the mountains;
A sudden F-stop change as a cloud drifts over the sun,
The interval helps me see earlier years for what they were—
Potent understandings, miserable misunderstandings, all in one click.
The wind picks up, abutting my face, forcing me to breathe,
Choice is not an option.
But in every life, options are chosen,
Even if one decides not to decide.

Gathering, ominous clouds in the western sky
Abut the ground, showing visual vertical clues to where rain falls,
Portending its future direction. Ah, but here my legs,
My trees, abut perpendicular to the ground,
Walking in utter defiance of impending change.
Incongruous mix of radiant-dagger sunshine and subtle-gunshot clouds
Grow into thunderstorms and abut peripheral panoramas;
Ah, but isn't life's warmth and clarity tempered with cold and vague notions?
Aren't we meteorologically mercurial? The one constant in life is change.

Enhanced Walk

At 7:00 a.m., I looked out my window to see cloudy skies but for a sliver of sun between cloud formations. It was as if the sun were playing peek-a-boo. I drove to the bluffs for my morning walk, determined to walk two miles on the path. Although it was cloudy, one could easily see Mt. Whitney, Mt. Breckenridge, and Bear Mountain. This was spectacle enough; however, it was also possible to see the Tehachapi Mountains to the south and Coastal Ranges to the west. As a child, I could see this all the time, however, as time passed, it was a rare treat to see all at once. As I got to the first bend in the path, walking west, I turned my head to the left to notice how the clouds had changed. They were light purple and as I looked across my left shoulder, I saw the sun trying to break through. Around the sun were clouds that had feathery white touches to them. They made the sun look as if it were shining through an opening surrounded by clouds made brighter than the rest. I continued my walk west to the trail's end, and then turned to walk east. At the halfway point in that leg of the walk, I looked up to see a solitary white bird fly north, and then fly west toward me. I never stopped walking, it never stopped flying. It wasn't flying very high, maybe eight to ten feet above me. It looked very white, like a dove and too small to be a gull. It looked down at me, I looked up at it and for a moment we were transfixed, and then off it flew, and on I walked. Before it made a turn, I noted it was in the same portion of the sky that I'd earlier seen the sun surrounded by feathery clouds. My two-mile walk had enhancements and awakenings today.

My Odyssey

Cardio Man

Seasons cycling, heart pumping, it's a toasty beginning
To a winter solstice observance;
Seventy degrees of close warmth
Perking nipples to a winter salute and
Bathing the lungs with the warm airs
Of Yule toxicity and unrefined JOY—
Jack Frost won't be nipping at these buds today.

Thanksgiving MMV

I take a mile-long walk on strange paths
Exhaling a gift to plants, they don't care if you have bad breath as
long as you breathe;
I am thankful for their gift of oxygen.
Energized I return to chums on Bishop Lane
Giving them a better man;
I am thankful for their tolerance.
A session of Pilates on the ball
Giving myself flexibility as hummingbirds mock my slowness
With their impossibly graceful speed and agility;
I am thankful for their occasional sight-line encounters.
An autumn day in California giving a refreshing pause—
I am thankful, grateful, and fortunate
To be a part of so many gift exchanges.

Four Letters to the Editor of the
Bakersfield Californian

"Learn to take care of your own pets"

I've read in recent letters about problems with cats and dogs. Neighbors complain about cats allowed to run through the neighborhood. Others complain about dogs that get loose and kill cats. Neither animal should be allowed the run of the place. These are not the plains of Africa where wild animals stake their territory.

If you talk to dog owners, they will undoubtedly blame the cat owners; if you talk to the cat owners, they undoubtedly blame the dog owners. My questions are two:

When did we decide to license and attempt to control canines and not felines?

When did we decide that dogs can run free within city limits?

An argument can be made that dogs bite and they decorate yards with awful-looking gifts. Cats don't? Try working in your garden and discovering one of their gifts.

An argument can also be made that that dogs can kill other things. Ahem . . . cats stand similarly accused.

Finally an argument can be made that dogs carry disease and fleas. Hmm . . . cats guilty as charged.

I sense an arbitrary bias toward dogs here. Cats can and should be kept in their own yards on their own property, just as dogs should.

Owners have a vital interest in controlling their pets. We often complain about government intrusion into our lives, but when we don't take the responsibility, that can be an open door to a governmental entity's solution.

All arguments aside, all opinions to the contrary, it is up to each of us to take responsibility for our own. If we are unable to take care of pets, how in blazes do we take care of humans?

"Many aspects improve children's education"

A *Bakersfield Californian* editorial this summer contended "the fewer students the better." It dealt with Bakersfield City School District's success with smaller classes in grades K-3. District officials Don Murfin and Dale Russell believed that smaller class sizes have a bearing on improved test scores. The editorial concluded with Murfin stating that we need to reduce class sizes in grades 4–6.

However, that's going to cost money to accomplish. Are taxpayers willing to part with more of their income in order to build and maintain a 1:20 teacher-to-student ratio in every K–6 classroom?

Test scores would, I suspect, improve in all grades given a 1:20 teacher-to-student ratio or lower. I doubt they would show consistent improvement on a K–6 campus that holds over five hundred children.

In any case, there is much more to a child's education than a score on a standardized academic test. There is much more to a child's education than how well they've mastered a particular district's grade-level standards. There is much more to a student's education than the report card.

All of these have their place, yet none of them will ever take over the importance of the roost. Parents are their children's first and foremost teachers and as such should be held to just as strict an accountability as teachers, administrators, board members, and legislators.

Yet I see no standardized testing being given to parents before they have children, nor is it a requirement for them to take a certain number of hours to keep their parenting credentials current.

"Return of wallet welcome surprise"
I recently had the misfortune of losing my wallet. All I could remember in the backtracking exercise of where it might be was that I had stopped to satisfy a craving at Smith's Bakery on Union Avenue.

After a stressful evening wondering if a piece of my mind had been lost with the wallet, I made a call to this bakery asking if someone had turned it in. I expected a no.

When the courteous woman answered yes, I hastened to the bakery where a sturdily-sealed envelope with my name on it was given to me.

She explained that a customer discovered it in the parking lot. I took the envelope home and checked the contents. Everything was as I had left it, including some of my Christmas shopping money.

In a season where giving is emphasized, we sometimes overlook kindness. To the person who returned my wallet to the bakery, thank for your kindness; to the people at the bakery who kept the item for me until I could figure out where it was, thank you also.

There are good folks living in this town!

"Money rules"
An earlier writer opined that we no longer have elections that select leaders "who will follow the standards of the founders of our country."

That got me wondering. I doubt that in this country's infancy that there was much heed given to things like "war chests," "sound bites" (or bytes come to think of it), or "media saturation."

I wonder what would happen to the election process if a candidate with no war chest or the smaller war chest won. Does money really buy a good leader? Minus wads of money to spend on sound bytes, would a prospective leader be more likely to communicate in depth with any improved efficacy?

Minus media saturation, would a candidate be able to speak without a media-driven image of him or herself? Although there's lots of money in the parties, I'm not certain the voting public ever gets what it pays for.

If individual and corporate contributors could contribute a maximum of one dollar to support the candidate, the proposition, the bond measure, etc., might there be a difference? Would the voters get any less than what they see and hear now?

The standards of the founders, whatever they encompassed, certainly left big money out. Maybe there was a reason for that. Do vote; perhaps that makes a difference.

There's no implied guarantee, but at least you can be heard.